Home-Hunt Like a Genius

The smart home-buyer's guide

by Shawn Fehily

SHAWN FEHILY

www.ShawnFehily.com

Dedication

I would like to dedicate this book to my soon-to-be-wife, Kathrine, whom I will marry as soon as I can get her through underwriting. Yes, that is mortgage humor. Not usually a funny business but I guess I am not your usual mortgage guy.

SHAWN FEHILY

Introduction

Hi and welcome to my little book about home hunting. I dearly love helping my clients buy their home whether it is your first home, family expansion, vacation home, investment property, or any other property configuration you need to finance. This book is written to serve you by becoming better informed about the home-buying process. Over time I will expand this book into further volumes as I continue to find more solutions to helping you with your dream home(s).

This book is written with one point per page so that there is room at the bottom of most pages for you to doodle while you make your rounds in search of your perfect place.

My very best,
Shawn

1: Where to start.

87% of all property search begins online so it is most likely you will start there, but where? Who has the most accurate representation of what is for sale or rent. Zillow is the biggest but their data is not live, meaning it is not pulling directly from the multiple listing service in most cases. Realtor.com is the true MLS data but they are just farming out leads to agents. Realtor.com is part of the National Association of Realtors which is the industry body but they are not a brokerage, they just send leads to their broker members. Redfin.com is MLS data with their own agents but they are not in every market. Homes.com provides data and software to the industry and generates leads for agents. Trulia is owned by Zillow and gets its data straight from brokers but again, not directly from MLS feeds.

2: Value

Price per square foot is the major measuring stick for value initially but most sites do not give you a simple way to search for this. Finding out what the market price per square foot is in the market where you are searching is step one. Then you have a benchmark for value which can be swayed by various factors such as condition and location. If the PPSF is $100 below market but you need to renovate you need to calculate the renovation cost. If you are buying the worst house on the best block (a winning strategy) there is some serious location upside to consider.

3: Data.

There is a lot of intelligence that can be gained from quality data. For example, if you see a concentration of distressed properties (pre-foreclosure or foreclosure, for example) this is usually an indication that the area's socio-economic demographic is quite low. With quality geo-spatial data, you can get an instant snapshot of nearby schools, restaurants, amenities and generally establish a solid overview of the neighborhood.

4: Listing quality.

If somebody wants to go to the trouble of selling their home and only have one (usually low quality) picture uploaded this says something about how the home may have been kept and the quality of the property. Sometimes real estate agents are simply lazy and just upload one image but usually it reflects the owner's enthusiasm in that property. There should be 10 images and a floor plan and they should be high enough resolution to see full screen. Sometimes you see a very expensive property with one low quality image. This can mean that the agent must list it but they do not want other agents enquiring. This is an attempt to keep the buy side and sell side commission. Rather than distributing the property as widely as best as possible, the agent tries to attract the buyer directly even though it is against their fiduciary responsibility to the seller they are representing.

5: When to engage agents?

With the availability of listings online, the need for an agent at the very beginning is significantly reduced. You can now research every property available yourself and gain significant insight autonomously. You may be comfortable to reach out to listing agent directly which they will certainly appreciate because they will be getting both the buyer side commission and the seller side simply because you don't have an agent representing you. The problem with this is of course that you don't have an agent representing you. The sellers-agent has a fiduciary responsibility to the seller so even if they have what is called dual agency (representing both parties) the whole idea of negotiating price is fundamentally undermined. Of course, you can represent yourself if you are comfortable. In most states the transaction is handled by the attorney so representing yourself is very achievable, however, there are distinct advantages of inside-local-knowledge and expertise.

6: Making an offer.

The process for making an offer varies from state to state but the psychology is the same. Before deciding on a number, you need to weigh up certain factors like how long the property has been up for sale. The longer they have been trying the more flexible they may be. Also, use other factors to justify a lower price. The most important of these is comparable (comps). By researching the price per square foot of everything in the area you can use the argument that the price per square foot needs to be lower. Some sellers won't care and hold firm but if you present a logical case people will often listen to reason. Of course, if you have an agent they will do all this for you and advise you along the way. Or at least they should.

7: Choosing where to live.

You probably have some driving factor influencing your decision like job or school proximity but if not how do you decide on a neighborhood? I suggest a zip code comparison tool where you can compare multiple factors like affluence, demographics, crime, and schools etc. Usually people like a neighborhood because they have come to know it and /or have friends living there, but coming into a new city can be overwhelming. A lot of people decide to rent first until they get a feel for the place which is a wise move.

8: Schools

When school is a deciding factor, which it is for most new parents, you need to understand what to look for. You can't really go on word of mouth too much because a school can have average academic scores but parents who have had kids attending the school for some time may favor it over others just from their experience. Results speak volumes and sometimes it is best to remove emotion and simply look at the facts.

9: Transport

If you a relying on public transport, obviously, proximity to stations is a major factor to consider. Map based search systems do a very good job of this, presenting you with a visual snapshot of the entire geo spatial landscape of the neighborhood. This is much more difficult on text based search applications but there are some good tools out there for these systems as well.

10: Common charges

When buying condos or co-ops there are maintenance charges to consider. Common charges are fees paid to the building each month, in order to manage it effectively. If these fees are above average it usually indicates that the building has a lot of debt. Most buildings are managed by management companies and there are well defined boundaries for expenses, so if the maintenance is high you need to look further into the reasons.

11: Property taxes

In certain cities like New York there are tax abatements that are put in place to stimulate development. These can significantly reduce the amount of your property taxes for up to 25 years. The first thing to look for is the standard property taxes for the zip code so you can determine if the property of interest is high or low. If the building has been diligent with the management of the taxes (many employ attorneys to argue the amounts with the city) they can be kept to a minimum but if left untended the taxes can be prohibitive.

12: What can you afford

Up until recently it was impossible to get pre-approved for a mortgage online but now, companies like guaranteed rate are offering this service. Being pre-approved for a mortgage is helpful in the buying process for two reasons. You are realistic about what you can spend and you can tell the seller that you are pre-approved for the amount required. Confidence is everything when negotiating a deal. The only thing better than being pre-approved is to be in a position to purchase with cash. Cash buyers are always preferred because the seller knows that it can close much faster with far less bureaucracy.

13: What is considered affordable?

Fannie Mae recommends that buyers spend no more than 28% of their income on housing costs. Go much past 30% and you risk becoming house poor. Being smart about this is a good way to create wealth. Putting what you would have spent on a bigger house into other property investment or otherwise repurposing in order to generate a return on investment.

14: Closing Costs

What many buyers forget to calculate are the closing costs required in purchasing a home. These costs include origination fees charged by the lender, title and settlement fees, taxes and prepaid items such as homeowner's insurance or homeowner's association fees. There are often even more hidden costs that are there to shock you at the closing table but everything should be disclosed on what is called a good faith estimate in advance of the closing. If you are not offered one of these just ask your attorney for one. It is usually provided by the lender and all costs are disclosed to the best of their knowledge although it is not the final that will be on the HUD1.

15: The Hud 1

This is a document attached to every property sale and it lists all the details of the transaction. It gets its name from Housing and Urban Development and it denotes who gets paid what down to the last cent.

16: Rent or buy economics.

Speaking of investment, sometimes property taxes, house maintenance and mortgage interest make it a more economical decision to rent. On the downside you are not building wealth via capital growth in the property but if you are on the edge of affordability at least you won't get smothered by unexpected costs, mortgage rate rises and real estate taxes. Sometimes it is better to have more headroom by waiting an additional year or two.

17: Inspections

Are you covered when you get your home inspected? A home inspector's job is to conduct a visual examination of the physical condition of the house and systems within it. They won't be pulling up carpets to make sure the floors aren't warped, for example, or drill into walls to check for insulation. Most homes have imperfections, and inspectors probably won't catch everything. They're looking for major defects — electricity that's not grounded, air-conditioning or heating systems that are unsafe. Get it inspected for sure but understand it is not a guarantee and it is not a magical x-ray of the home.

18: The motivation of Home inspectors.

In many cases home inspectors rely on agents to get their leads so it stands to reason that the inspector may be more loyal to the longstanding agent relationship than the one off buyer. Hire your own. Beware the referral.

19: Keep Your Money Where It Is.

It's not wise to make any large purchases or move your money around three to six months before buying a new home. You don't want to take any big chances with your credit profile. Lenders like to see that you're reliable and they want a complete paper trail so that you qualify for the best loan possible. If you open new credit cards, amass too much debt or buy a lot of big-ticket items, you're going to have a hard time getting a loan or at least a good rate.

20: Get Pre-Approved for Your Home Loan.

There's a big difference between a buyer being pre-qualified and a buyer who has a pre-approved mortgage. Anybody can get pre-qualified for a loan. Getting pre-approved means a lender has looked at all your financial information and they've let you know how much you can afford and how much they will lend you. Being pre-approved will save you a lot of time and energy so you are not running around looking at houses you can't afford. It also gives you the opportunity to shop around for the best deal and the best interest rates. Do your research: Learn about junk fees, processing fees or points and make sure there aren't any hidden costs in the loan.

21: Avoid a Border Dispute

Knowing precisely where your property lines are may save you from a potential dispute with your neighbors. Also, your property tax is likely based on how much property you have, so it is best to have an accurate map drawn up. This just requires getting a survey done on your property so you know exactly what you're buying.

22: Timing the Market

So many buyers try to time the market and figure out when is the best time to buy. Trying to anticipate the housing market is very difficult. The best time to buy is when you find your perfect house and you can afford it. Real estate is cyclic, it goes up and it goes down and it goes back up again. So, if you try to wait for the perfect time, you're probably going to miss out. Find the perfect house instead.

23: Bigger Isn't Always Better

Everyone's drawn to the biggest, most beautiful house on the block. But bigger is usually not better when it comes to houses. The rule is don't buy the biggest, best house on the block. The largest house only appeals to a very small audience and you never want to limit potential buyers when you go to re-sell. Your home is only going to go up in value as much as the other houses around you.

24: Buy it, don't date it.

Buying a house based on emotions is just going to break your heart. If you fall in love with something, you might end up making poor financial decisions. There's a big difference between your emotions and your instincts. Going with your instincts means that you recognize that you're getting a great house for a good value. Going with your emotions is being obsessed with the paint color or the backyard. It's an investment, so stay calm and be wise.

25: Stalk the hood

Before you buy it's good to get the lay of the land – drop by morning noon and night. Many homebuyers have become completely distraught because they thought they found the perfect home, only to find out the neighborhood wasn't for them. Drive by the house at all hours of the day to see what's happening in the neighborhood. Do your regular commute from the house to make sure it is something you can deal with on a daily basis. Find out how far it is to the nearest grocery store and other services. Even if you don't have kids, research the schools because schools affect the value of your home significantly.

26: Grants and subsidies

Researching if there are grants that apply to you is an easy enough process. Start with a google search for state or federal government home buyer grants. There is often something you can take advantage of.

27: Close or move on

If you're able to work out a deal with the seller, or better yet, if the inspection didn't reveal any significant problems, you should be ready to close. Closing basically involves signing a ton of paperwork in a very short time, while praying that nothing falls through at the last minute.

28: Costs

Things you'll be dealing with and paying for in the final stages of your purchase may include having the home appraised (mortgage companies require this to protect their interest in the house), doing a title search to make sure that no one other than the seller has a claim to the property, obtaining private mortgage insurance or a piggyback loan if your down payment is less than 20%, and completing mortgage paperwork.

29: Retirement or bust

It is not a good idea to rely on making a killing on your home to fund your retirement.

Even though you own a home, you should continue to save the maximum in your retirement savings accounts each and every year. Although it may seem hard to believe for anyone who has observed the fortunes some people made during the housing bubble, you won't necessarily make a killing when you sell your house. If you want to look at your home as a source of wealth in retirement, consider that once you've paid off your mortgage, the money that you were spending on monthly payments can be used to fund some of your living and medical expenses in retirement.

30: When to sell

The best time to think about selling your house is before you buy it. Be sure that the home you buy has features other buyers will find desirable, or you won't be able to get a good price when you sell it.

31: Over capitalizing

Everybody wants to improve their home but there is a point where you are spending money without increasing value. This may be because what you are building has limited appeal for potential future buyers or because the house will be valued on square footage no matter what you think your new handball court and waterfall may be worth. Whenever possible, add square footage. Nobody argues with feet. Of course, you may find a buyer who is passionate about handball which will add emotional connection to the purchase but will only slightly lift valuation in standard valuation metrics.

32: Renovations that make sense

Kitchens add value both perceptually and tangibly. Hardwood doors, granite bench tops and high quality appliances are sometimes the easiest way to improve a home's appeal. If you are buying and you are not happy with the kitchen, you can allow a minimum of 20,000 to rectify which can be a good negotiating tactic. Especially if the seller agrees that the kitchen is sub-par.

33: Meet the neighbors

Neighbors are a wealth of information. They will freely share all sorts of knowledge about the neighborhood, the amenities and even the person you are buying from. Neighbors will usually be very nice to you if you say you are thinking of buying the house next door. And if they are not nice to you, they might make bad neighbors. Again, important information.

34: Check the traffic noise.

When you are excited about a property it is easy to ignore subtleties so it's a good idea to measure them against a base line. Most mobile devices now have apps that can measure decibels. While you are in the home why not take a few readings and compare to where you live now to get some perspective.

35: Why not buy next to a cemetery?

Well actually, there is an argument that supports buying next to a cemetery and that is simply "dead people make great neighbors". Now if you are planning on selling at some point you probably need to consider whether this will narrow the buyer market but you could always use it as a selling point. For example, "2 Bedroom home with beautiful grounds and the quietest neighbors in the world". You will probably get a deal on the place too. Just be careful around Halloween.

36: Squeaky stairs

Well built stairs don't squeak so that is often a key performance indicator on a home's build quality. Plus, you just don't want to live with squeaky stairs.

37: Upstairs foot steps

If you can, get someone to walk heavily or jump on the floor above you. If the home is well built you should hardly hear anything. If corners have been cut you will hear every step. Quality multi story homes have sound insulation measures built in.

38: Looks like rain

Most people don't look for homes in the rain so you can very easily be fooled into thinking the house is water proof. Check the ceilings carefully for water damage, warping, discoloration or fresh paint. And if you are really serious, come again when it's pouring cats and dogs.

40: Gutter ball

If possible, check the gutters and see if they are clear. People who look after homes clean gutters. It's often left to the least priority so if the gutters are clean you have a good chance that the home is well maintained in general. Home inspectors are not looking for these subtleties but they tell important stories about the owner.

41: Bricks

Bricks are great but mortar gets old. Often, buildings of a certain age need to be pointed. Pointing is a process of removing mortar brick by brick and replacing it. It is very costly so make sure you check carefully.

42: Shingles

Everybody loves the shingle look but be prepared to be treating it against the weather on a regular basis. An important factor to add to you projected maintenance budget.

43: Dogs

Check the neighbor's yards for dogs. Dogs are great but they get excited. Sometimes they get excited endlessly about anything that happens. People moving. People not moving. Cars, ducks, squirrels, wind. Almost anything can set off dogs and if they surround you, you had better be a dog person and a person that does not mind barking. Dogs barking that is. You probably don't bark, yourself. If you do, make sure the neighbors like dogs too.

44: Water pressure

Hardly anyone checks the shower. Just turn it on and see what's what. If you like water pressure and the home's is weak it can get expensive to remedy.

45: Level best

Take along a small spirit level. You would be surprised how few homes are level in every room and sometimes you can pick up problems with foundations if one room is particularly sloped. Floors and tops of doors give you a good indication of the home's overall levelness. Dirt and foundations settle over the years leaving tables that can roll a pencil.

46: Sink or swim

Check under the sink for water damage. Leaky pipes are easily fixed but again it is a very good indicator of the owner's degree of attention to maintenance.

47: Attic

Most owners don't expect an attic visit and attics tell all sorts of stories. Check the corners for pest evidence, check for signs of moisture and check for cleanliness. Clean attics mean attention has been paid.

48: On tap?

Tap the wood on exterior windows with something that has a little weight. If the sound is not solid there could be rot or pest damage. Of course, the inspector will check this but why hire an inspector to inspect a house that you have already found to have problems.

49: Check the internet bandwidth.

If you work from home or just like fast downloads, then make sure you have plenty of bandwidth available in the internet service provider. It seems obvious but so many people do not check and regret later.

50: Room to rent

If you are having trouble with affordability you could consider searching for a home with a separate or separate-able structure like a garage that could be modified so you could subsidize your mortgage payment by renting out a room.

51: Not all tenants are equal

If you are going to rent the room, try renting it to somebody useful. A plumber, a policeman or some sort of handy person. At the very least someone who is willing to contribute to the work load of maintaining a property in return for a break in the rent. Out of 10 applicants, some will be far more useful than others.

52: Buy the building

It's not nearly as crazy as it sounds. If there is an apartment building with 5 – 10 apartments you can probably achieve certain economies of scale that will give you an apartment of your own at very little cost because you are leveraging the rental income of the other apartments. Often you can easily syndicate the purchase by having multiple investors come in with you. If you find the right building you can return an attractive percentage to investors while enjoying a reduced living expense. Obviously, this is not for everyone but if you like the idea of owning a building it is worth considering.

53: 1031 exchange.

This is more for the property investor but when you sell a property and make a sizeable profit you are going to be taxed capital gains. If you use the proceeds to buy another property immediately you are not taxed. This is called a 1031 exchange. Alternatively, you can use a service that invests your proceeds into a portfolio of properties so you do not have the burden of ownership and management but maintain the upside of capital gain and monthly dividends.

54: Power outages

There is nothing more annoying than blackouts and some areas are far more susceptible to them than others. There are many online services that document outages but asking stores in the area is very effective as they are badly affected when the power goes out. If you love the area but power outages occur regularly, there are standby generators you can install that trip on automatically as soon as the power goes out. These can be a very valuable investment and you can also use it as negotiation leverage if it is a high outage neighborhood.

55: Profit is often made at the purchase

Money is made when you buy not when you sell. Buying a house is far easier than selling one and an important lesson to learn is that you make the most money when you buy the house. What this means is if you buy the right house on the right street at the right price, you have already set yourself up for a win when you sell. The theory rings true when buying anything and it is an economically smart way to think.

56: Lucky numbers.

Sometimes you can increase your buying audience just by having the right street number. It does not hurt to do a quick study on numerology because there is a surprising number of people who consider this when buying. For example, the number 888, considered to be a number that attracts wealth, if preceded by a 6 it multiplies the effect. So, house number 6888 could well attract a Chinese buyer or someone who considers numerology important.

About the author

Shawn Fehily was born near Philadelphia and moved to Texas at age 5 with his family. As a Marcus High School attendee, Shawn played football on the 5-a Texas state champ team graduating with honors in 1998. Having applied to only one college, Penn State, and being immediately accepted, Shawn called the dean and asked for a deferment of 1 year in order to work and study in Germany where he became fluent in the language. Summers at Penn State saw Shawn interning in the mortgage industry which firmly established his background and post-Penn he accepted a full-time position as a loan officer. Now a Senior Loan Officer and Mortgage loan specialist, Shawn has over 14 years of high level corporate experience in the home loan industry. Shawn is a Dallas local and enjoys life with his fiancé (soon to be wife and probably is by now), 3 dogs, family nearby and plays an active role in the community.

www.ingramcontent.com/pod-product-compliance
Lightning Source LLC
Chambersburg PA
CBHW071639040426
42452CB00009B/1699